NATIONAL GEOGRAPHIC

# How Does My Bike Work?

Jan McPherson

I am riding my bike.
Look at how my bike works.

I push down on one pedal.
I push down on the other pedal.
I make the pedals go around.

3

When I make the pedals go around,
they turn a big sprocket.

chain

big sprocket

4

When the big sprocket goes around,
it turns the chain.

pedal

5

When the chain goes around,
it turns a small sprocket.

small sprocket

chain

6

back wheel

When the small sprocket goes around,
it turns the back wheel.
When the back wheel goes around,
my bike moves forward.

7

When I need to turn,
I turn the handlebars.

When I turn the handlebars,
the front wheel turns.
My bike turns.

When I squeeze the brake lever,
the brake pads press against the tires.
My bike slows down.

brake lever

brake pad

tire

This is how my bike works.

# Glossary

| | |
|---|---|
| brake lever | small bar on handlebars that operates the brake pad |
| brake pad | pad that presses against the tire to slow down the bike |
| chain | metal links joined together |
| handlebars | metal bar with handles that steers the bike |
| pedals | levers pressed by the feet to operate the bike |
| sprocket | circle of metal teeth that fits into a chain |
| tire | covering around a wheel |
| wheel | round object that turns |